The Way of the Stoic

Epictetus

Also by Gary W. Cross

Exploring the Way of Epictetus
Exploring the Way of Jesus
Exploring the Way of the Buddha
Exploring the Way of Lao Tzu
Exploring the Way of Epicurus

The Way of Sophia with Humps in Mind
Exploring Wisdom with Humps in Mind
Exploring a Good Life with Humps in Mind
Exploring the Mind – Discovering Humps and How they shape us

By Gary Cross and Cheryl Cross

The Way of Sophia circa 2017
Exploring a Way to a Good Life
Exploring Wisdom

The Way of the Stoic

Epictetus

A Short Introduction

Gary W. Cross

ISBN-13: 978-1979864008

ISBN-10: 1979864004

December 2017

Cover: The Ancient Roman theatre in Hierapolis, the city where *Epictetus* was born.

Credit: Cover photograph by Antoine Taveneaux (2011) 'Ancient Roman theatre in Hierapolis.' from: https://commons.wikimedia.org/wiki/File:Theatre_in_Hierapolis.jpg

Credit: Publishing logo by Sophie

The Way of the Stoic Epictetus301117.docx

For Chez

For what is it that all people seek? To be calm, to be happy, to do all as we desire, not to be hindered, not to be compelled.

CONTENTS

Preface

Epictetus[a] deserves to be heard.

It is by listening to *Epictetus* that we best learn the way of the ancient Stoics.

Listening to *Epictetus*, we become aware of our ways (our beliefs, concepts and behaviours) that have been shaped by the ancient Stoics.

Listening to *Epictetus*, we learn of a way that offers much that can still help us to improve our own way to a better life.

This book is part of the series *Ways of the World* in which I explore different ways of the world that have helped to shape my mind, and I suggest, the minds of many in the world today.

This series also includes the book *Exploring the Way of Epictetus*, in which I allow *Epictetus* to explain in greater detail the way of the Stoic. Compared to this book, *Exploring the Way of Epictetus* includes: more topics; more quotations; and footnotes that give the original Greek words and their meanings.

My aim in this current book, *The Way of the Stoic Epictetus* is to present a short, easily assimilated overview of the way of the Stoic as espoused by *Epictetus*.

---

[a] *Epictetus* (Greek: ἐπίκτητος) is pronounced *E- pik - te - tus*. *Epictetus* means: in addition; something newly acquired; worth getting or desirable.

Acknowledgements

I have been very fortunate to have Cheryl's help when writing this book. Cheryl has provided comprehensive feedback which ranged from pointing out formatting, spelling and grammatical errors through to comments and discussions about the book in general.

This book would be very much the poorer without her assistance.

Stoicism
The meaning of this
word hardship without
showing ones feelings

Introduction

Epictetus was born in about 55 CE in Hierapolis (adjacent to Pamukkale in present day Turkey). Hierapolis was of ancient Greek heritage and culture, but in *Epictetus'* time it was part of the Roman province of *Asia*. He was born a slave (his parents were slaves). At some time, he moved to Rome where he was a slave to Epaphroditos, a freedman and secretary (*a libellis*) to the Roman Emperor Nero. He studied Stoic philosophy while still a slave. At some time, Epaphroditos gave *Epictetus* his freedom. After attaining his freedom, he taught philosophy in Rome before being banished by Emperor Domitian (along with other philosophers) in 89 CE. *Epictetus* went to Nicopolis, the then capital of the Roman province *Epirus-vetus* (an area in north-western Greece). *Epictetus* continued to teach Stoic philosophy in Nicopolis until he died aged 80 (c135 CE).

Stoicism was a dominant philosophy in the ancient Greek and Roman world for over 800 years (from approximately 300 BCE to approximately 500 CE). During that period, Stoicism influenced all levels of society from slaves (for example, *Epictetus*) to Emperors (for example, *Hadrian*[a] and *Marcus Aurelius*[b]).

The Greek philosopher *Zeno*[c] is credited as being the founder of Stoicism. However only fragments of his works, and those of other early Stoics, have survived. Indeed, it is to the works of the later Stoics, *Seneca*[d], *Epictetus* and the Roman Emperor *Marcus Aurelius*

---

[a] *Hadrian* (76 – 138 CE), Roman Emperor from 117 to 138 CE. Hadrian was said to have formed a friendship with *Epictetus* and to have had visited him at Nicopolis.

[b] *Marcus Aurelius* (121 – 180 CE), Roman Emperor from 161 to 180 CE. In *Meditations* Marcus states that he was given a copy of *Epictetus' Discourses* by one of his teachers (Rusticus). He frequently quotes *Epictetus* in his *Meditations*.

[c] *Zeno of Citium* (334 – 262 BCE). Zeno taught in Athens in a *Stoa* - a covered walkway, which usually had columns on one side – thus he and his students became to be known as Stoics.

[d] Lucius Annaeus Seneca (c. 4 BCE – 65 CE), tutor and advisor to the Roman Emperor Nero.

that we must turn to find surviving texts of ancient Stoic philosophers. However, I suggest that it is to the works of *Epictetus* that we best turn to understand Stoicism. The works available today by *Seneca* and *Aurelius* were personal exposés and were not intended to be discourses on Stoic philosophy. Whereas, the works of *Epictetus'* are focused on espousing Stoic philosophy, and thus more closely reflect the way of the Stoic.

The structure of this book

A way should tell us about: **the destination** that it leads to; any **problems** that may interfere with us reaching the destination; **directions** that will help us to reach the destination; and **strategies** that will assist us to overcome any problems and help us to successfully follow the directions.

So, in the first chapter, my aim is to share with you what I discovered to be the destination that *Epictetus* suggests we all seek. Next, I present the problems that *Epictetus* suggests impedes us from reaching the destination. Next, I present the directions that *Epictetus* offers to help us to reach the destination. And finally, I present the strategies that *Epictetus* offers to help us to successfully follow his directions and to cope with any problems that we may be encounter.

A collection of flowers

Ideally, I would let *Epictetus* speak for himself and present a collection of *Epictetus'* words (that is, an anthology, which literally means a collection of flowers). However, nothing that *Epictetus* personally wrote survives today. However, one of his students, *Arrian*[a], recorded *Epictetus'* discourses or lectures:

> 'I neither wrote the words of Epictetus in the manner in which men write such things, nor did I make them public myself, any more than I wrote them. But whatever I heard him say, that I tried to write down in the very same words, so far as possible, to preserve as reminders for my own use of his thinking and frankness.'

---

[a] Arrian of Nicomedia (86 – 160CE) born in Nicomedia (in present day Turkey) was a Roman administrator, consul, legate, historian and philosopher.

And thus, it is from Arrian's *The Discourses of Epictetus*[a] that I source *Epictetus*' words.

A note on the translations

Arrian wrote *The Discourses of Epictetus* in an ancient form of Greek known as *Koine*[b] Greek, which was the language used throughout the eastern Roman Empire for administration, trade and other general use. The quotations are my own translations from the Greek versions of *The Discourses of Epictetus* available today[c].

A note on how I translate the Greek word λόγος: λόγος is usually translated as 'reason' but this does not convey to us today the divine dimension that people in the Hellenistic period would have associated with the word. *Epictetus* tells us (in 1.3.1-3) that people consisted of two parts, the body which we had in common with animals, and a divine part which we had in common with the gods; and that our divine part consists of λόγος and our mind. Christians would be familiar with the divine aspect of λόγος, for example, in the first verse of *John* (where λόγος is translated as 'Word'): 'In the beginning was the Word (λόγος), and the Word (λόγος) was with God, and the Word (λόγος) was God.'

To retain this divine dimension, I leave λόγος untranslated, but use the Romanised *logos*.

---

[a] Arrian's *The Discourses of Epictetus* was written and circulated before Epictetus died and thus it is probable that *Epictetus* was aware of the books and indeed may even have had some 'editorial' input. Only four of the original eight books of *The Discourses of Epictetus* are now remaining. *The Discourses of Epictetus* was written in ancient Greek (*Koine*).

[b] *koine* (*koinos* common, shared in common; common to all people, public). Thus, *Koine* Greek was common Greek or the form of Greek, at the time, used for common use, for example, when trading.

[c] In *Exploring the Way of Epictetus,* I include footnotes that give, for key words in the quotations, the original Greek words and their meanings and varied nuances. The footnotes help you to understand how I arrived at my translations.

1

THE DESTINATION – calm, happy, free, desires met

Arrian tells us that 'when he (*Epictetus*) uttered them (his discourses), it was clear that he had no other purpose than to move the minds of those listening to what is best.'

Epictetus tells us that to achieve the best is to:
: Be happy
: Be calm, tranquil and without passion
: Attain what we desire
: Avoid our aversions
: Be without pain or fear
: Take care of our duties to family and fellow citizens
: Be successfully progressing
: Be pious
: Be free

'For the God has made all people to be **happy**, to be **calm**.' [3.24.2]

'For those putting it together, out of this {the work of the philosopher} results in **not failing to attain desires**, and **not falling into aversions**, **leading to being without pain, without fear, calm** and concerning himself with the community **taking care of the relationships** both the natural and acquired, child, father, as a brother or sister, citizen, man, woman, neighbour, companion, ruler or being ruled.' [2.14. 8]

'And now I am your teacher, and you are instructed in my school. And I have this purpose, **to make you unhindered, unconstrained, free from interference, free, successfully progressing, happy,**

looking to the God in everything small and great. And you are here to learn and to practise these things…' [2.19.29]

The destination in summary:

The destination *Epictetus* wants us to reach is one where we are *happy, calm, attain what we desire, avoid our aversions, are free, are without pain or fear, take care of our duties to family and fellow citizens, successfully progressing, and are pious.*

This is a rather long definition of the destination. Thankfully, in the following quotation, ***Epictetus* offers a summary of the destination** he wants us to reach, namely, the destination is one where we are *calm, happy, do all we desire, and are free* (not to be hindered, not to be compelled).

'For what is it that all people seek? **To be calm, to be happy, to do all as we desire, not to be hindered, not to be compelled**.' [4.1.46]

Perhaps *Epictetus* had in mind that *to do all we desire* covers both *attaining what we desire* and *avoiding our aversions*; and that *being happy* covers: *being without pain and fear, looking after others, taking care of our duties to family and fellow citizens, successfully progressing, and being pious*. That is, *Epictetus* implies that we can't be happy if: we are experiencing pain or fear; if we are not looking after our family and fellow citizens; if we are not progressing; and if we are not pious.

In short, the destination that *Epictetus'* helps us to reach is one where we are **calm, happy, free, and our desires are met.**

And thus, I turn to *Epictetus* to tell us more about being calm, happy, meeting our desires, and being free.

¤ *Calm*

'What then have I need of? ...to be **calm**, **to have a mind in accordance with nature, to not have an agitated mind**.' [3.9.17]

Epictetus to tell us that unless you seek calmness, tranquillity and apathy (freedom from emotion)[a], then you are not a true philosopher:

'...you who in name only have come to philosophy... you who have not ever sought **calmness**, **tranquillity**, and **apathy**.' [3.26.13]

¤ *Happy*

Epictetus tells us that if we look always to Zeus[b] when we are doing something, then we will always be happy:

'... Zeus is the father of men... and to him only he looked at when he was doing what he was doing. Therefore, it is in his power to be always **happy**. [3.24.16]

Epictetus goes on to tell us that we can never be happy if we have unsatisfied desires:

'But it is never possible to have happiness and desire for what is not present, for to have full happiness one must have all that one desires... [3.24.16-17]

---

[a] Apathy meant: to have no pathos, no passion or feelings or emotion, impassionate, freedom from emotion, tranquil

[b] Ζεύς father and ruler of the gods and men; often referred to as The God

¤ *Desires met*

Central to *Epictetus'* philosophy is ensuring that our desires are satisfied, and our aversions avoided. Without achieving these *Epictetus* tells us that we will fail to successfully progress, and fail to be calm and happy:

'The one making progress… having learned that successful progress and apathy only prevail in the man who does not fail to gain what he desires, and whose aversions are not embraced;' [1.4.1]

'… this is the greatest proof of misfortune and unhappiness: to wish for something and it does not happen; and … not to wish for something and it happens;' [2.17.18]

¤ *Free*

Epictetus tells us that we are free when we are not compelled, hindered, constrained or impeded; when our wishes and desires are fulfilled; and when our aversions are avoided:

'**He is free who** lives as he wishes, and who is **not compelled** and **not hindered**, and **not constrained**; whose actions are not impeded, whose desires are attained, and who avoids aversions.' [4.1.1]

Epictetus also tells us that to be free is to be free of passion, pain, fear and mental disturbances:

'For the things (you are) taking care of (are) not trivial: **respect and trust and calmness, apathy, freedom from grief, freedom from fear, tranquilness, put simply, freedom.** [4.3.7-8]

'**Does freedom seem to you good? The greatest**! Then is someone who is attaining the greatest good able to be unhappy or to act badly? No. Then whoever you see unhappy, progressing unsuccessfully, (or) lamenting, you can confidently declare that they are not free.' [4.1.52]

THE DESTINATION – in summary

The destination that *Epictetus* helps us to reach is one where we will:

¤ Be happy
¤ Be calm, tranquil and without passion
¤ Attain what we desire and avoid our aversions
¤ Be without pain or fear
¤ Take care of our duties to family and fellow citizens
¤ Successfully progress
¤ Be pious
¤ Be free

The destination in essence: one where we are **calm, happy, free, and our desires are met.**

2

PROBLEMS - faulty thoughts

Epictetus tells us that the problems that stop us from being calm, happy and free are:

¤ Our desires for, and aversions to, externals
¤ Our hastily reacting to perceptions;
¤ Identifying with our body
¤ Our faulty thoughts

¤ *Desires and aversions for externals*

Epictetus reminds us that we feel unfortunate, unhappy and wretched when we don't get what we desire or when we get what we seek to avoid:

'... **this is the greatest proof of misfortune and unhappiness: to wish for something and it does not happen; and ... not to wish for something and it happens; who is more wretched than I**?' [2.17.18]

Epictetus tells us that it is because we have **desires and aversions for externals** that we often fail to fulfil our desires and often fail to avoid our aversions:

'**What do we admire? Externals. About what things are we eager about? About externals.**' [2.16.11]

Epictetus goes so far as to say that all our difficulties are due to externals:

'**All difficulties for people are due to externals**...' [4.10.1]

Epictetus uses the word 'externals' to refer to anything external to our mind, for example: our body; our possessions; others' thoughts, words and actions. Externals are not under the control of our will, but rather, things under the control of others, nature or the gods. Will as we may, but we will still fall ill, still age, and still eventually die; still lose our possessions; and still not be able to control what others think, say and do:

'In our power are volition and all the works (resulting from our) volition; **things not in our power are the body, the parts of the body, possessions, parents, brothers or sisters, children, country, put simply, the things we have in common with others.**' [1.22.10]

With this understanding of externals, we can now return to the problem of having **desires and aversions for externals**:

'To indulge your desire (for) wealth and aversion (for) poverty: you will fail to attain (the desire), you will embrace (the aversion). But **you will be unfortunate (also in desiring)** health, power, honours, country, friends, children, in a word to **anything not under the control of the will**.' [2.17.24]

'**You seek successful progress and happiness where they are not... Why do you seek this in externals**? It is not in the body... It is not in possessions... It is not in power...' [3.22.26-30]

Epictetus suggests that not satisfying our desires and not avoiding our aversions are the main reason we are not calm:

'... **for an emotion is produced in no other way except whenever (we are) failing to attain a desire or embracing an aversion**. This (results in) the disturbances of the mind, tumult, no fortune, the bringing of bad fortune, grief, lamentation, ill-will, the making of envy and jealousy, and because of these we are not able to listen to *logos*.' [3.2.3]

And *Epictetus* suggests that not satisfying our desires and not avoiding our aversions are the main reason we are not free:

'Is it possible for someone desiring anything that is in the power of others to be unhindered? No. Is it possible to be free from interference? No. Therefore, **he cannot be free**.' [4.1.64-65]

'...if {he believes his good and benefit is conferred} in things external and not under the control of the will, he by necessity is to be hindered, to be **put in bonds**, to be a slave to the person having the power over that which he admires and fears...' [4.7.10-11]

The first problem in summary:

: Having desires and aversions for externals - for things we do not control.

¤ *Hastily reacting to perceptions*

The second problem that *Epictetus* identified is our **hastily reacting to perceptions**:

'...**anything appears, and straightway I act on that appearing... And what kind of tragedy has any other beginning**? ... And what is said of those chasing after everything appearing? They are being insane.' [1.28.30, 32-33]

Epictetus tells us that when we allow our experiences to happen by chance, and then react without consideration of what we perceive, we are failing:

'But **the one (to respond to) the perceptions to be experienced by him randomly and fruitlessly and as chanced upon**, and to not attend closely to *logos* nor proof nor sophism, nor put simply, to discern, by questioning and answering, the things of his concern and not of his concern, and **is not all of this a failing**?' [1.7.33]

Epictetus tells us that the only cause of pain is our hasty thoughts:

'**And put simply, neither death nor exile nor pain nor anything else like this is the cause of us doing or not doing anything, but (our) hasty judgement and thoughts**.' [1.11.33]

Epictetus tells us, no greater storms affect us than the storms in our minds arising from strong perceptions:

'For of **what kind of storm is greater than the one arising from perceptions (that are) strong and expels *logos***? [2.18.29]

The second problem in summary:

: Hastily reacting to perceptions-
- Being impulsive
- Getting distracted
- Not thinking before we react

¤ *Identifying with our body*

Epictetus tells us that people consist of two parts, our animalistic body and our divine part, which consists of *logos* and our mind; and that **problems occur when we identify with our body** rather than with our divine part:

'…these two things are mixed in the creation of us, the **body** in common with the animals, and ***logos*** and **the mind** in common with the gods - while few (are inclined) towards the divine and happy (that is, with the mind), others are inclined towards the unfortunate and dead relationship (that is, with the body) …' [1.3.3]

Epictetus tells us what we identify with becomes our master:

'Where the 'I' and the 'mine', there the animal by necessity inclines: if in the flesh, there is the master: if in the volition, it is there: and if it is in externals, there.' [2.22.15, 19]

Epictetus tells us that when we identify with our body we behave inappropriately like wild beasts:

'**Because of this relationship {with the flesh} they are inclining to become like wolves**, untrustworthy and treacherous and harmful, and (like) the lions, savage and brutal and untamed; but the greater number of (are like) foxes, and as other misfortunate animals.' [1.3.7-8]

'**Beware then that you do nothing like a wild animal; but if not, you have destroyed utterly the human**, you have not fulfilled (your) promise. (Also) beware (that you) do nothing like a domesticated animal; but if not, also in this way (you) destroy utterly the human. What then do we do as domesticated animals? Whenever (we act) on account of the belly; or the sex organs; or randomly; whenever (we act) sordidly; or inconsiderately; where are we inclined towards? Towards the domesticated animals. What have we destroyed utterly? That with *logos*. Whenever combative, harmful, passionate and impetuous, where are we inclined towards? Towards the wild animals.' [2.9.3-7]

The third problem in summary:

: Identifying with our body

When we identify with our body (our animalistic part) we behave like a beast (not divinely, which we are capable of).

¤ *Faulty thoughts*

The fourth problem that *Epictetus* identified is **our faulty thoughts**.

Epictetus tells us that our thoughts cause everything that we do, say, feel, desire and avoid:

'... **it is always the same that which is the cause of anything we do and not do, of anything we say and not say, of being elated or being dejected, of avoiding or pursuing anything...** And what is this? Indeed, **is it other than that which thinks for us**? **No other.**' [1.11.28, 30]

And thus, when we do, say or feel something inappropriate, it is due to nothing else other than our thoughts:

'**Therefore, when we may be doing anything not rightly, from this day we shall accuse nothing else than the thoughts**, from which we have done this...' [1.11.34-35]

'And so, in this way **the great and terrible works have their origin in** this: (how) things appear to **the mind**? This and no other.' [1.28.11]

Epictetus tells us that because it is our thoughts that make our acts shameful or virtuous, it is a person's thoughts that must be judged not whether they appear inferior or common (that is, don't judge someone by their externals):

'**You should never praise or censure (someone) because of their being common, but because of their thoughts**. For these are one's own, the things which makes one's acts shameful or virtuous.' [4.4.44]

Epictetus reminds us that the noble, the strong, the rich and the beautiful also suffer because of their faulty thoughts:

'...**the noble, the strong, the rich, the beautiful**, when they do not have the kind of thoughts there is need of, **are not prevented from being wretched and unfortunate**...' [4.10.36]

The fourth problem in summary:

: Faulty thoughts are ultimately the problem - faulty thoughts shape faulty actions (including reactions), words, feelings, desires and aversions.

THE PROBLEMS – in summary

Epictetus tells us that the problems that stop us from reaching our destination are:

¤ Desires and aversions for externals
¤ Hastily reacting to our perceptions
¤ Identifying with our body
¤ Faulty thoughts

And given that our faulty thoughts are ultimately the problem:

The problems in essence: our faulty thoughts.

3

EPICTETUS' DIRECTIONS – be a philosopher

Epictetus tells us that if we wish to overcome the problems that stop us from being calm, happy, free and from satisfying our desires, then we should follow the way of the philosopher:

'And **why have you come to the philosophers**[a]? ... **in this way you will be calm and without fear**.' [4.1.83-84]

Epictetus tells us that it is by being a philosopher that we overcome our faulty thoughts and make 'our *logos* right':

'For this is the preconception of a philosopher... to have a worn-out cloak and long hair... **What then is the matter of the philosopher**? Is it not a worn-out cloak? No, **it is nothing but *logos***. **What is his aim**? Is it not to wear a worn-out cloak? No, it is nothing but **to make his *logos* right**.' [4.8.6, 12]

---

[a] Φιλόσοφος: philosopher, friend or lover of wisdom, loving learning and knowledge, one who investigates and discusses the causes of things and the highest good

But *Epictetus* tells us that the way of the philosopher is not easy:

'Do you think that doing these (what you do now) you will be able to be a philosopher? Likewise, do you think that you will be able to eat (as you do now), likewise drink, similarly to be angry, similarly to be displeased? You will need to be attentive, to work hard, to conquer any desire, to depart from family, to be looked down upon by children, to be laughed at by those meeting you, in all to be inferior, in power, in honours, in custom. Having considered these, if it (still) seems good to you, **come to (philosophy), if you wish to exchange these for apathy[a], freedom, tranquillity**.' [3.15.10-12]

So, what does being a philosopher entail? *Epictetus* tells us that to be a philosopher we need to follow these directions:

¤ **Have desires and aversions only for what we can control**
¤ **Accept what we can't control**
¤ **Test perceptions before assenting to them**
¤ **Identify with and use our divine part**
¤ **Be virtuous – act in accordance with our divine part.**

[a] Remember that apathy meant: to have no pathos, no passion or feelings or emotion, impassionate, freedom from emotion, tranquil

¤ *Have desires and aversions only for what we can control*

The first direction *Epictetus* tells us to follow to be calm, happy and free is to **have desires and aversions only for what we can control**.

Epictetus tells us that if we have desires and aversions for externals (for things that we can't control), then we will fail to attain our desires and avoid our aversions:

'If you do not wish to desire something that may fail to hit the mark nor to have an aversion for something that one may fail to avoid, **desire nothing that belongs to others** (that is, nothing that others, including the gods, have the power over) and **have aversions for nothing that is not in your power**. But if not, by necessity (your desires will) fail to hit the mark and (your aversions will) be embraced.' [4.10.6]

And if we fail to attain a desire or avoid an aversion, we will not be calm:

'…for **an emotion is produced in no other way except** if **failing to attain a desire or if embracing an aversion**.' [3.2.3]

And *Epictetus* tells us if we have desires and aversions only for what we can control, we will not only ensure that our desires will be met and our aversions avoided, but we will also achieve freedom:

'…**who is unhindered? The one desiring not one thing that belongs to others…** [4.1.129]

Epictetus tells us that happiness is found in us (in our own mind):

'**You seek successful progress and happiness**… **you would find it being in you, not in being led astray by externals and not in seeking what belongs to others as one's own**.' [3.22.26, 38]

Epictetus goes even further suggesting that we should restrict all our concerns and all our attention to things of the mind. All else, *Epictetus* suggests, is 'naught to us':

'The things we have been eager about, these no one has power over; **those things which others have the power over, these we pay no attention to**. What kind of trouble can we still have?' [1.25.1-2]

'...indeed **he removes the desire (for externals) out of him all together and sets himself above** (them), and (has desires and) aversions only towards things which are subject to the will. For if he avoids anything perchance not under the control of the will, he knows that at some time he will embrace the thing for which he has an aversion and will be unfortunate.' [1.4.1-2]

'And because of this, **if indeed in these things alone he believes his good and benefit is conferred, in the unhindered and on these absolutely, then he will be free, successful, happy, without harm, generous, pious, having gratitude to God for all things, by no means finding fault with nothing happening, accusing nothing...**' [4.7.9]

The first direction in summary:

: Have desires and aversions only for what we can control - not for what we can't control (externals).

In doing so, our desires will be satisfied, our aversions avoided; and we will be free and calm.

¤ *Accept what we can't control*

The second direction *Epictetus* tells us to follow is to **accept what we can't control**, that is, accept externals. Importantly, *Epictetus* tells us that if we truly accept externals (as they are and not as we may otherwise desire them to be) then we will have no desires and aversions that are not in harmony with the externals - our desires will be satisfied, and our aversions will be avoided (and we will be calm and free).

'And here we present the work of the philosopher to be something like this, **that one must fit our will to what is happening**, so that neither any of the things happening happens against our will, nor the things not happening do not happen as per our wishes.' [2.14.7]

'First then we must have these principles at hand, and do nothing apart from these, but to have directed the psyche to this end: **to pursue nothing external, nothing belonging to others; but** (to pursue only) **as the one having the power decrees, all the things under the control of the will, otherwise as the things perchance may be offered.'** [4.12.15]

The second direction is to accept what we can't control, namely, others, nature and God. Thus, in the following quotations, *Epictetus* tells us that this direction includes the need to:

: Accept nature as it is, and be in harmony with nature
: Accept God, and be in harmony with God.

Accept nature and be in harmony with nature

As part of the second direction to accept what we can't control, *Epictetus* emphasizes the need to accept nature. To accept nature is to have our desires and aversions in harmony with nature and thus, to act in accordance with nature:

'But much more important is the **law of life - to act in accordance with nature**. For if in all matters and circumstances we wish to attend to things in accordance with nature, it is clear that in everything we must aim neither to flee from that which is in accordance with nature, nor to accept that which is in conflict with nature.' [1.26.1-2]

'Whenever someone has their proper stasis in life, he does not gape in eager expectation at externals. Man, what do you wish to have? Indeed, **I am satisfied when: I reach out for and turn away from things according to nature, seek and shun as is natural**...' [1.21.1-2]

Accept God and be in harmony with God

Another part of the second direction is to accept God, and to have our desires and aversions in harmony with God's wishes:

'**The philosophers say that it is first necessary to learn this, that there is God**.' [2.14.11]

'... dare to look up to the God to say that hereafter **use me as you wish**; I am of the one mind as you; I am like you; **I shun nothing that you expect (of me); where you wish, lead (me)**... [2.16.41-42]

'What has he (God) given to me (that is) mine and in my own power, (and) what has he reserved for himself? **He has given to me the will, in the power of me to do, unimpeded, unhindered**... Why then fight against God? Why wish for the things not (able to) wish for, the things not being offered to us out of everything (that is possible) to have? But how? As it has been offered and for as much as it is able.' [4.1.100-101]

'... and put simply **wish for nothing other than that which the God wishes**. And who will hinder you, who can compel you? Certainly no one more than Zeus. When you have a leader such as this, and you have the same wishes and desires, why do you still fear failing?' [2.17.22-23]

'**Who then is a Stoic**? … Someone show me the psyche of a person wishing **to be of one mind with the God, and who does not blame either God or man, nor fail to attain anything, nor embrace anything, who is not angry, envious, or jealous -** (why indeed be indirect?) **who is desiring to be transformed from a man to God and (who,) in this poor dead body of theirs, is resolved to have fellowship with Zeus**. Show me! [2.19.23, 26-27]

***The second direction in summary*:**

: Accept what we can't control, including-
- Accept and be in harmony with nature
- Accept and be in harmony with God.

¤ *Test Perceptions*

The third direction that *Epictetus* tells us to follow is to **test perceptions** before acquiescing to them.

'**The most important and first task of the philosopher is to test perceptions** and to distinguish them and to use none which is untested.' [1.20.7]

'And where is your work? … **in purpose and pausing, in order that (you are) not deceived**.' [1.4.11-12]

'For as Socrates said an unexamined life is not to live, so **an unexamined perception is not to be accepted**' [3.12.14]

Epictetus tells us that the goal is to ensure our perceptions are in accord with nature, that is, that we desire what is good, reject what is bad, and are indifferent to all else:

'… the work of the virtuous and good person is **to want their perceptions to be in accordance with nature**… to move with desire towards the good, and to turn away from the bad, and neither of the two ways towards that which is neither good nor bad… From this every motion of people and of the gods is dependent upon.' [3.3.1-2, 4]

Epictetus tells us that it is with our divine part (our *logos* and mind) that we examine the perception:

'I (Zeus) have given to you a portion of something of us, this power of both seeking and shunning things and of both reaching out for and turning away from things – put simply, **knowing how to use the perceptions of things**…' [1.1.12]

Epictetus tells us that if what we perceive is not under our control, then it is of no concern to us:

'What have you perceived? ... **Apply the rule:** (Is it) **not under the control of the will or under the control of the will?** (If it is) **not under the control of the will**: Remove (it) out! ... Throw it away, (it is) nothing to you.' [3.3.14-15]

The third direction in summary:

Test perceptions before acquiescing to them:
: Think before reacting.

¤ *Identify with and use our divine part*

The fourth direction *Epictetus* tells us to follow is to **identify with and use our divine part** (our *logos* and mind).

Epictetus tells us that we, like the gods, are children of the God (Zeus), and accordingly should be elated. Yet most people identify with their non-divine part (their body) and thus are unfortunate:

'... **from the God**[a] **we have all come into existence and that the God is father of humans and the gods** ... and if you know that **you are a child of Zeus**, will you not be elated? And yet we are not so; since these two things are mixed in the creation of us, the body in common with the animals, and ***logos*** **and the mind in common with the gods** - while few (are inclined) towards the **divine and happy** (that is, with our divine part), others are inclined towards the unfortunate and dead relationship (that is, with the body) ...' [1.3.1-3]

Epictetus tells us that although our body may be insignificant when compared to the cosmos, our *logos* is great and equal to that of the gods:

'(Do you) not know, how small a part (you are) in comparison to the whole? But this (is) in reference to the body; in reference to ***logos*** **(you are) not at all inferior to the gods**, not more trivial; for the greatness of *logos* is not judged by length and not by height, but by thoughts.' [1.12.26]

Epictetus tells us that although plants and animals, like us, are made by the God, plant and animals are not part of the God. Unlike the plants and animals, we have a divine part (our *logos* and mind),

---

[a] τοῦ θεοῦ: the God; Zeus. [*Epictetus* speaks of God (singular) and gods (plural). God singular refers to Zeus, father and ruler of the gods and men.]

and that it is when we are using our *logos* and mind that our divine part shines:

'Are they (plants and animals) not works of (the) gods? They are, but (they do) not proceed logically and (they are) not parts of (the) gods. But **you are proceeding logically, you are a piece of the God**[a], you have something in yourself (that is) part of him. Why then do you not know of your relationship? ... Wretch, you carry God and you don't know.' [2.8.10-12]

Epictetus suggests that if we believe that we share *logos* with God, and that God is the good, then it is in *logos* that we should seek the good:

'The God is beneficial; and also the good is beneficial. It is likely then, where the essential nature of the God is, there is also the essential nature of the good. **What, then, is the essential nature of God?** Flesh? No way! Land? No way! Fame? No way! (It is) **intelligence**, **knowledge**, **right *logos***. Plainly therefore seek here the nature of the good. Surely then you do not seek this in plants? No. Not in anything without *logos* (animals)? No.' [2.8.1-4]

Epictetus tells us that when we believe that the good is to be found in that which is unhindered (namely, our mind) then we will be free, successful and happy:

'... **if indeed in these things alone he believes his good and benefit is conferred, in the unhindered and on these absolutely, then he will be free, successful, happy**...' [4.7.8]

But if we believe that the good is found in externals (things not in our power) then we will become slaves:

'...if {he believes his good and benefit is conferred} in things external ... he by necessity is to be hindered, to be put in bonds, to be a slave...' [4.7.10-11]

---

[a] τοῦ θεοῦ: the God; Zeus. [*Epictetus* speaks of God (singular) and gods (plural). God singular refers to Zeus, father and ruler of the gods and men.]

'How then is someone to take care of tranquillity and calmness... **The first thing and the work of life is this: distinguish the things of importance and separate them and say the externals are not in my power; choice is in my power. Where do I seek the good and the bad? Within the things (that are) mine** (our mind).' [2.5.2, 4-5]

***The fourth direction in summary*:**

: Identify with, and use, our divine part - our *logos* and mind

¤ *Be virtuous – act in accordance with our divine part*

The final direction that *Epictetus* tells us to follow is to **be virtuous**. And *Epictetus* tells us that if we identify with our divine part (our *logos* and mind) and act accordingly then our behaviour will be virtuous.

Epictetus constantly reminds us that while we have a mortal part (like animals) we also have *logos* (our divine part), and to act as a human is to act in accordance with *logos*:

'**For what is a human? The answer is a mortal animal with *logos***. Frankly then from what does (having) a *logos* separate us? From wild animals. And from what others? From domesticated animals and like animals. Beware then that you do nothing like a wild animal; but if not, you have destroyed utterly the human, you have not fulfilled (your) promise.' [2.9.2-3]

Epictetus tells us that we must reference everything that we do otherwise we will act randomly, and possibly wrongly:

'**First say to yourself who you wish to be**: so then do what you have to do … For everything that we do, if we refer it to nothing, we will do it randomly; and if (we refer it) to that (which is) not right or proper, (we will do it) wrongly. **Finally, there is a universal reference, and a personal reference**. **(The) first (reference is) as a human**. What does this encompass? Not (to be) like a domesticated animal, whether harmful or gentle; nor like a wild animal. And **the personal reference (is concerned with) each person's way of life and the volition (the mind)**.' [3.23.1, 3-5]

Epictetus tells us that because we have a divine part that we share with the gods, when we learn the nature of the gods we also learn what our own divine nature should be:

'The philosophers say that it is first necessary to learn this, that there is God… The next (thing to learn is) of what nature are they (the gods)? For such as they are found to be, **the (person) who**

would please and obey them must attempt with (all his or her) power to be like them. If the divine is trustworthy, and so this (person) to be **trustworthy**; if free, and so this (person) **free**; if (does) beneficial work, and so this (person) **beneficial work**; if generous, and so this (person) **generous**; therefore thereafter everything the (person) does and says is as **an emulator of God**.' [2.14.11-13]

Epictetus tells us that our divine nature is to be modest, trustworthy, exalted, undaunted, free from passion and calm:

'He (Zeus) has given over yourself to you and says, 'I have none other more trustworthy than you: keep this (person) for me such as he is by nature, **modest, trustworthy, exalted, undaunted, free from passion and calm**.' [2.8.23]

***The fifth direction in summary*:**

: Be virtuous - act in accordance with our divine part.

EPICTETUS' DIRECTIONS – in summary

Epictetus tells us that to reach the destination (to be calm, free, have our desires met…) we need to be a philosopher; and that to be a philosopher we need to follow five directions:

¤ **Have desires and aversions only for what we can control**.
¤ **Accept what we can't control**, including:
: Accept and be in harmony with nature
: Accept and be in harmony with God
¤ **Test perceptions** before acquiescing to them:
: Think before reacting.
¤ **Identify with and use our divine part** (our *logos* and mind).
¤ **Be virtuous** – act in accordance with our divine part**.**

***Epictetus*' directions in essence: be a philosopher**.

4

EPICTETUS' STRATEGES

Epictetus offers the following strategies to help us to cope with the problems, to follow our directions, and ultimately, to reach our destination:

¤ **Education - gain knowledge**
¤ **Practice**
¤ **Pause - don't be impulsive**
¤ **Start our now.**

¤ *Education - gain knowledge*

The first strategy *Epictetus* offers is to seek **education** - to gain knowledge.

Epictetus tells us that we must learn how to follow the directions, and ultimately, how to reach the destination:

'**Your purpose was to furnish yourself knowledge of** how to use, according to nature, the perceptions presented to you; in having unerring desires, and in not falling into aversions, never unfortunate, never bad luck, free, unhindered, unconstrained, conforming to the administration of Zeus, trusting in this, being well pleased in this, finding fault with nobody, accusing nobody, being able to say from your whole psyche the verse *Lead me, O Zeus, and indeed you Destiny*'. [2.23.42]

Epictetus tells us that part of what we must learn is what is in our control and what is not:

'And **to be educated, this is to learn the things (that are) one's own and the things (that) belong to others**.' [4.5.7]

'And what else have you been studying from the beginning than to distinguish the things yours and not yours, the things in your power and not in your power, the things hindered and unhindered?' [4.1.83]

Epictetus suggests that the first thing necessary to learn is of the existence of God:

'The philosophers say that it is **first necessary to learn this, that there is God**[a] and he provides for the whole (the universe) …' [2.14.11]

---

[a] τοῦ θεοῦ: the God; Zeus. [*Epictetus* speaks of God (singular) and gods (plural). God singular refers to Zeus, father and ruler of the gods and men.]

Next, *Epictetus* suggests we need to learn the nature of the gods in order that we may learn how to ensure our own nature is divine:

'**The next {thing to learn is} of what nature are they {the gods}**. For such as they are found to be, the (person) who would please and obey them must attempt with (all his or her) power to be like them.' [2.14.11-12]

Epictetus tells us that we also need to study the acts and administration of the God (Zeus) in order that we may be in harmony with the God (for example, we need to learn the patterns of the world around us, which *Epictetus* would have believed, were the result of actions by the God):

'Thus he considers and reflects, that, if he attaches himself to the God, he will pass through (life) safely. How do you mean to be attached? When, the (God) wishes, he wishes also, when the (God) does not wish, he does not wish. How then may this happen? For how otherwise than by **examining the acts and the administration of the God.**' [4.1.98-100]

Similarly, *Epictetus* tells us that our education needs to be about how we can follow the gods; how to be contented with their administration; and how to be free:

'The one being educated ought to come to be educated with this notion: 'how can I follow the gods in everything, and how shall I be contented with the administration of the gods, and how can I become free?' [1.12.8]

In the same vein, *Epictetus* tells us that we need to study nature (the acts of the God) in order that we may learn how to be in harmony with nature:

'But **to be educated is this, to learn to wish every time in this way: as it happens.** And how do things happen? As the one decreeing decrees them. He has decreed summer to be and winter... Remembering then this decree, **we must go to be instructed**, not in order that we may change the basic principles - for that is not given to us – but **in order that in this way (we are) possessing the (knowledge) concerning us, as things are and have been formed by nature, (and that) we may have the mind of itself conforming to the things taking place**.' [1.12.15-17]

'That is **why above all we need education**, so as to learn to adapt our preconception of what is reasonable and unreasonable **to be in harmony with nature**.' [1.2.6]

And since our mind is part of the gods, *Epictetus* tells us that we should also learn about our mind:

'**From today therefore (every) day we will consider and examine nothing else**, of what nature something is or in what manner it is, not the field not the slaves not the horses or dogs, **but our thoughts**... You see then that you must become a scholastic, this being who all deride, if indeed you wish to do investigation of your own thoughts. And that this is not for one part of the day or day, just think on this! [1.11.38-40]

***Epictetus*' first strategy in essence: Education.**

We need to gain knowledge about:
: What is, and is not, in our control
: The gods - so that we can be in harmony with them
: Nature - so that we can be in harmony with nature
: Our own mind

¤ *Practice*

The second strategy *Epictetus* offers is to **practice**.

Epictetus tells us that it is not enough to learn how to be a philosopher, but we also have to practice it. Without practice our old habits will continue and we will not have changed for the better:

'**Each (person) is strengthened and preserved by appropriate acts** ... Because of this, **philosophers exhort us not to be satisfied with only learning**, **but also to** take in additional study and exercises, then **practice.'** [2.9.10-13]

'Every habit and ability is maintained and strengthened by the corresponding acts, the (habit) of walking by walking, the (habit) of running by running. If you wish to be a good reader, read: if a writer, write... Generally then **if you wish to make something a habit, do this; if you do not wish to make something a habit, don't do it**, but accustom (yourself) to do something else instead of this... The same sort of thing happens with the passions of the psyche... If then you wish not to be angry, don't feed the habit, throw nothing on it causing it to increase. First you should keep quiet and count the days when you were not angry.' [2.18.1-2, 4, 11-12]

'And what is it that being set before us to practice? (How) to live with desires and aversion unhindered. And what does this mean? Not failing to attain (what is) being sought, and not falling into (what is) being avoided. Towards this then the exercises must be inclined. For since **it is not (possible) to have an unerring desire and to not fall into an aversion without great and continuous exercise,** know that, if you permit to divert this to externals - to the (things) not under the control of the will - you will not have the desire obtained and the aversion avoided.' [3.12.1, 3-5]

Epictetus' second strategy in essence: Practise!

: Practice what we have learnt - learning is not enough
: Without practise we do not change our habits
: Without practise we do not get closer to our destination

¤ *Pause - don't be impulsive*

The third strategy *Epictetus* offers is to **pause** - to not be impulsive.

Epictetus has told us that one of the causes of our tragedies is our hastily reacting to perceptions, and that we need to test perceptions before we assented to them. In order to be able to test perceptions, *Epictetus* tells us that we need to pause before assenting to them:

'For as Socrates said an unexamined life is not to live, so an unexamined perception is not to be accepted, **but say, 'Wait**! (That) I may see (if) you are permitted' [3.12.14-15]

'(If) you oppose this (perception) you will conquer the perception, you will not be drawn by this. **First do not be seized and carried away by the quickness (of events), but say 'Wait for me, perception!** Go away (so that) I can know what you are and what (you are) about, go away (so that) I may test you.' And hereafter don't yield to it to lead the way - painting a picture of what happens next. If not, it will rush you along carrying you where it wishes.' [2.18.24-25]

Epictetus tells us that it takes much effort to ensure that we don't get seized and carried away by perceptions:

'This is the true athlete the one exercising himself against such perceptions. **Stay, wretch, do not be seized and carried away (by the perceptions).** Great is the struggle, divine the work, for control, for freedom, for successful progress, for tranquillity.' [2.18.27]

Epictetus' third strategy in essence: Pause!

: Pause before reacting to perceptions - don't be impulsive
: Without pausing, we get swept along by perceptions

¤ *Start out now*

The fourth strategy *Epictetus* offers is to **start out now**!

Epictetus tells us to not wait before we start on our journey; that we need to decide immediately, with all our mind, whether to continue to be a slave or to be free:

'For when you are subjected to your externals, you become a slave hereafter and do not resist. (Do not) on the one hand sometimes desire to be a slave and on the other hand sometimes desire not (to be a slave), but **simply with the whole of the mind either (be) this or that:** (choose) **either freedom or slavery**, either (to be) educated or uneducated... But if these (for example not being free) (are) causing shame, **now decide immediately**...' [2.2.12-14]

Epictetus tells us that we need to be desperate to reach the destination:

'**Be desperate now** for successful progress, for freedom, for nobleness of mind.' [2.16.41]

Epictetus' fourth strategy in essence: Start out now!

: Choose now if you wish to be a slave or to be free
: If you wish to be free start out now!

EPICTETUS' STRATEGIES – in summary

The strategies that *Epictetus* offers to help us to follow his directions and reach his destination include:

¤ **Education - gain knowledge**
We need to gain knowledge about:
: What is in our control
: The gods - so that we can be in harmony with them
: Nature - so that we can be in harmony with nature
: Our own mind

¤ **Practice**
: Practice what we have learnt - learning is not enough
: Without practise we do not change our habits

¤ **Pause - don't be impulsive**
: Pause before reacting to perceptions - don't be impulsive
: Without pausing we get swept along by perceptions

¤ **Start out now**
: Choose now if you wish to be a slave or to be free
: If you wish to be free, start out now!

THE WAY OF EPICTETUS – a summary

DESTINATION – calm, happy, free and our desires met

The destination that *Epictetus* helps us to reach is one where we will:

¤ Be happy
¤ Be calm, tranquil and without passion
¤ Attain what we desire and avoid our aversions
¤ Be without pain or fear
¤ Take care of our duties to family and fellow citizens
¤ Successfully progress
¤ Be pious
¤ Be free

PROBLEMS

Epictetus tells us that the problems that stop us from reaching our destination are:

¤ Desires and aversions for externals
¤ Hastily reacting to our perceptions
¤ Identifying with our body
¤ Faulty thoughts

EPICTETUS' DIRECTIONS – be a philosopher

Epictetus tells us that to reach our destination we need to:

¤ Have desires and aversions only for what we can control
¤ Accept what we can't control, including:
  : Accept and be in harmony with nature
  : Accept and be in harmony with the God
¤ Test perceptions before acquiescing to them
¤ Identify with and use our divine part
¤ Be virtuous – act in accordance with our divine part

EPICTETUS' STRATEGIES

Epictetus offers the following strategies to help us:

¤ Education - gain knowledge
¤ Practice
¤ Pause - don't be impulsive
¤ Start out now

THE WAY OF EPICTETUS – *in essence*

¤ **Seek to be calm, happy, free and have our desires met**

¤ **Be a philosopher:**

: Have desires and aversions only for what we can control
: Accept what we can't control
: Test perceptions - don't be impulsive
: Identify with, think and act in accordance with our *logos* and mind
: Gain knowledge

Bibliography

Dobbin, R. (2008) *Epictetus – Discourses and Selected Writings* London: Penguin Classics

Liddell and Scott, (1889) *An intermediate Greek-English Lexicon.* Oxford: Oxford University Press.

Liddell, Scott and Jones *Greek English Lexicon* – sourced from *http://www.perseus.tufts.edu*

Long, George (translator) (1890) *The Discourses by Epictetus* - sourced from *http://www.perseus.tufts.edu* and *http://classics.mit.edu//Epictetus/discourses.htm*

Matheson, P.E. (translator) (1916) *Epictetus – The Discourses and Manual together with fragments of his writings* Oxford: Oxford University Press

Oldfather, W.A. (translator) (1925) *Epictetus – The discourses as reported by Arrian, The Manual and Fragments* Cambridge: Harvard University Press

Thayer, J.H., (1885) *The New Thayer's Greek-English Lexicon of the New Testament.* Peabody, Massachusetts: Hendrickson Publishers.

About the author

One of **Gary's** passions is to explore the mind and what shapes it. In the series, *Ways of the World* Gary explores different ways of the world that have helped to shape his mind – including religious, philosophical and secular ways. Books in this series currently include: *Exploring the Way of Jesus, Exploring the Way of the Buddha, Exploring the Way of Lao Tzu, Exploring the Way of Epicurus,* and *Exploring the Way of Epictetus* and this book *The Way of the Stoic Epictetus*. Other ways that have influenced Gary include science, psychology, engineering, philosophy, and more broadly, Western Culture.

Gary's other passions include: Cheryl (who he has had the great joy of being married to for more than forty years); their children and grandchildren; exploring a good life and wisdom (what they are and how to achieve them); reading (especially about philosophy, religions, science, psychology, technology, health and fitness…); running, health and fitness - and coffee with Cheryl.

Gary has tertiary qualifications in engineering, science (cognitive psychology) and religious studies.

Gary is also the author of:

Exploring the Way of Epictetus
Exploring the Way of the Buddha
Exploring the Way of Jesus
Exploring the Way of Epicurus
Exploring the Way of Lao Tzu
The Way of Sophia with Humps in Mind
Exploring a Good Life with Humps in Mind
Exploring Wisdom with Humps in Mind
Exploring the Mind - Discovering Humps and How they shape us

Gary and Cheryl are the authors of:

The Way of Sophia circa 2017
Exploring a Way to a Good Life
Exploring Wisdom

Printed in Great Britain
by Amazon

57768842R00037